The Baptism with the Holy Spirit

R.A. Torrey

A Modern Edition by Daniel Robison

Copyright © 2015 Daniel Robison

All rights reserved.

ISBN: 978-1508903987

Scripture quotations are from the ESV® Bible (The Holy Bible, English Standard Version®) copyright © 2001 Crossway, a publishing ministry of Good News Publishers. Used by permission. All rights reserved.

CONTENTS

1 WHAT IT IS AND WHAT IT DOES   1
2 THE NECESSITY AND OPPORTUNITY   11
3 HOW TO OBTAIN IT   20
4 REFILLED WITH THE SPIRIT   44
5 HOW SPIRITUAL POWER IS LOST   47

INTRODUCTION

Any honest reader of Scripture is forced to admit that the baptism with the Holy Spirit is indeed an experience verified by the writings of the New Testament, yet for many this topic remains one that is veiled in mystery. Controversy and confusion abound, and have so muddied the water that the critical skeptic finds ample reason to dismiss the topic entirely, and the sincere seeker can easily become overwhelmed and disheartened. Yet in the midst of all the controversy and confusion stands this little book, in which R.A. Torrey has masterfully composed what I would consider a guidebook on this topic that is straightforward, practical and biblical. This work is sure to serve as an invaluable aid to both skeptic and seeker alike.

In this updated edition, all scripture quotations have been changed from the Revised Version to the English Standard Version, with many of the scripture references moved to footnotes to keep the text as uncluttered as possible. There have been some changes to the original text where word usage and phrasing was outdated and could be confusing for the modern reader, but I have endeavored to preserve Torrey's original feel as much as possible.

My hope is that through this work the reader may personally experience for themselves that power of the Holy Spirit which the Father freely offers to all his children through Christ.

-Daniel Robison

CHAPTER 1

WHAT IT IS AND WHAT IT DOES

First of all we find that there are a number of names for this one experience in the Bible. In Acts 1:5, Jesus said, *"you will be baptized with the Holy Spirit not many days from now."* In Acts 2:4, when this promise was fulfilled, we read *"they were all filled with the Holy Spirit."* In Acts 1:4, the same experience is spoken of as *"the promise of the Father,"* and in Luke 24:49, *"the promise of my Father,"* and, *"clothed with power from on high."* By comparing Acts 10:44-47 with Acts 11:15-16, we find that the expressions *"the Holy Spirit fell,"* *"the gift of the Holy Spirit,"* and *"received the Holy Spirit"* are all equivalent to *"baptized with the Holy Spirit."*

Next we find that the baptism with the Holy Spirit is a definite experience—a man can know whether he has received it or not. This is clear from our Savior's command to the apostles: *"But stay in the city until you are clothed with power from on high."*[1] If this clothing with power, this baptism with the Holy Spirit, was not an experience so definite that a man could know whether he had received it or not, how could the apostles tell when those commanded days of waiting were at an end? The same thing is clear from Paul's very specific question to the disciples at Ephesus: *"Did you receive the Holy Spirit when you believed?"*[2] Paul obviously expected a definite "yes" or "no" for an answer. Unless this kind of experience was so definite that a man could know whether he had received it or not, how could these disciples answer Paul's question? In fact, they knew they had *not* received or been baptized with the Holy Spirit, and a short time later they knew they had received or been baptized with the Holy Spirit.[3]

Ask many men today who pray to be baptized with the Holy Spirit, "Well, my brother, did you get what you asked for? Were you baptized with the Holy Spirit?" and they would be confused. He did not expect anything so definite that he could confidently answer "yes" or "no" to a question like that. But in the Bible we find nothing of that vagueness and uncertainty which we find in much of our modern prayer and speech regarding this subject.

The Bible is a very definite book. It is very definite about salvation, so definite that a man who knows his Bible can confidently say "yes" or "no" to the question, "Are you saved?" It is just as definite about the baptism with the Holy Spirit. A man who knows his Bible can confidently say "yes" or "no" to the question, "Have you been baptized with the Holy Spirit?" There may be those who are saved and do not know it because they do not understand their Bibles, but it is their privilege to know it. In the same way, there may be those who have been baptized with the Holy Spirit who do not know the biblical name for what has come to them, but it is their privilege to know.

The baptism with the Holy Spirit is a work of the Holy Spirit that is separate and distinct from his regenerating work. To be born again by the Holy Spirit is one thing, but it is something further to be baptized with the Holy Spirit. This is clear from Acts 1:5. There Jesus said, *"you will be baptized with the Holy Spirit not many days from now."* At that point they were not yet baptized with the Holy Spirit, but they were already born again. Jesus himself had already pronounced them so in John 15:3, where he had said to the same men, *"Already you are clean because of the word that I have spoken to you,"*[4] and in John 13:10, *"And you are clean, but not every one of you."* The *"not every one of you"* excluded Judas Iscariot from the statement, *"you are clean"*—the one unregenerate man in the apostolic company. The apostles, except for Judas, were already born again at that point, but they were not yet baptized with the Holy Spirit.

It is obvious from this that being born again is one thing, and the baptism with the Holy Spirit is something different, something further. Someone can be born again and yet still not be baptized with the Holy Spirit. The same thing is clear from Acts 8:12-16, where we find a company of believers who had been baptized. Surely in this company of baptized believers there were some who were born again. But the record informs us that when Peter and John came down they *"prayed for them that they might receive the Holy Spirit, for he had not yet fallen on any of them."*

So it is clear that someone may be a believer, may be born again, and yet not have the baptism with the Holy Spirit. In other words, the baptism with the Holy Spirit is something distinct from and beyond his regenerating work. Not every man who is born again has the baptism with the Holy Spirit, though as we will see later, every man who is born again *can* have this baptism. If a man has experienced the regenerating work of the Holy Spirit he is a saved man, but he is not equipped for service until he has received the baptism with the Holy Spirit in addition to this.

The baptism with the Holy Spirit is always connected with testimony and service. Look carefully at every passage in which the baptism with the Holy Spirit is mentioned, and you will see it is connected with and is for the purpose of testimony and service.[5] This will come out very clearly when we consider what the baptism with the Holy Spirit does. The baptism with the Holy Spirit is not for the purpose of cleansing from sin, but for the purpose of empowering for service.

There is a line of teaching put forward by a very earnest but mistaken group of people that has brought the whole doctrine of the baptism with the Holy Spirit into disrepute. It goes like this: First, there is a further experience (or second blessing) after being born again—namely, the baptism with the Holy Spirit. This first proposition is true and can be easily proven from the Bible. The second proposition is that this baptism with the Holy Spirit can be received instantaneously. This proposition is also true and can be easily proven from the Bible. The third proposition is that this baptism with the Holy Spirit eliminates our sinful nature. This proposition is untrue. Not a line of Scripture can be cited to show that the baptism with the Holy Spirit eliminates our sinful nature. So the conclusion drawn from these three propositions, two true and one false, is necessarily false.

The baptism with the Holy Spirit is not for the purpose of cleansing from sin, but for the purpose of empowering for service. It is indeed the work of the Holy Spirit to cleanse from sin. There is also a work of the Holy Spirit which strengthens the believer with power in his inner being, that Christ may dwell in his heart through faith and that he may be filled with all the fullness of God.[6] There is a work of the Holy Spirit that sets the believer free from the law of sin and death,[7] and through the Spirit he puts to death the deeds of the body.[8] It is our privilege to walk this way daily and hourly in the power of the Spirit, with our fleshly nature being kept in the place of death. But this is not the baptism with the Holy Spirit, and the elimination of our sinful nature is not the baptism with the Holy Spirit, either. It is not something done once and for all, but something that must be maintained moment by moment. *"But I say, walk by the Spirit, and you will not gratify the desires of the flesh."*[9]

While insisting that the baptism with the Holy Spirit is primarily for the purpose of empowering for service, it should be added that the baptism is accompanied by a great increase in morality.[10] This is necessarily so because of the steps one must take to obtain this blessing.

We will get an even clearer and fuller view of what the baptism with the Holy Spirit is when we recognize what this baptism does. This is stated clearly in Acts 1:8: *"But you will receive power when the Holy Spirit has come upon you, and you will be my witnesses."* The baptism with the Holy Spirit imparts power—power for service. This power will not manifest itself in precisely the same way in each individual. This is brought out very clearly in 1 Corinthians 12:4-13: *"Now there are varieties of gifts, but the same Spirit...for to one is given through the Spirit the utterance of wisdom, and to another the utterance of knowledge according to the same Spirit, to another faith by the same Spirit, to another gifts of healing by the one Spirit, to another the working of miracles, to another prophecy, to another the ability to distinguish between spirits, to another various kinds of tongues, to another the interpretation of tongues. All these are empowered by one and the same Spirit, who apportions to each one individually as he wills."*

In my early study of the baptism with the Holy Spirit I noticed that in many instances those who were baptized in this way *"spoke with tongues,"* and I often wondered if everyone would speak with tongues when they are baptized with the Holy Spirit. But I saw no one speaking in this way, and I often wondered if there was anyone today who is actually baptized with the Holy Spirit. But 1 Corinthians 12 cleared me up on that, especially when I found Paul asking those who had been baptized with the Holy Spirit, *"Do all speak with tongues?"*[11] But I fell into another error—that anyone who received the baptism with the Holy Spirit would receive power as an evangelist or a preacher of the word. This is equally contradictory to the teaching of that chapter, which says that, *"there are varieties of gifts, but the same Spirit."*

There are three evils that arise from the mistake just mentioned. The first is disappointment. Many will seek the baptism with the Holy Spirit expecting power as an evangelist, but God has not called them to that work, and the power that comes from the baptism with the Holy Spirit manifests itself in them in another way. Many cases of bitter disappointment and almost despair have arisen from this cause.

The second evil is graver than the first—arrogance. A man whom God has not called to the work of an evangelist or minister rushes into it because he has received—or thinks he has received—the baptism with the Holy Spirit. Many men have said, "All a man needs to succeed as a preacher is the baptism with the Holy Spirit." This is not true. He needs to be called to that specific work, and he needs to study the word of God to prepare him for that work.

The third evil is still greater—indifference. There are many who know they are not called to the work of preaching. For example, a mother with a large family of children knows this. So if they think that the baptism with the Holy Spirit simply imparts power to preach, it is a matter of no personal concern to them. But when we come to see the truth that, while the baptism with the Holy Spirit imparts power, the way in which that power will be manifested depends upon the work to which God has called us. And when we come to see that no efficient work can be done without it, then the mother will see that she needs this baptism just as much as the preacher! She needs it for that most important and holy of all work—to bring up her children *"in the discipline and instruction of the Lord."*[12] I recently met a very happy mother. A few months ago she heard of the baptism with the Holy Spirit, sought it and received it. "Oh," she joyfully exclaimed as she told me the story, "since I received it, I've been able to get into the hearts of my children, which I was never able to do before!"

It is the Holy Spirit himself who decides how the power will manifest itself in any given case. The Holy Spirit *"apportions to each one individually as he wills."*[13] We have a right to *"earnestly desire the higher gifts,"*[14] but the Holy Spirit is sovereign, and he, not we, must ultimately determine the matter. So it is not our place to choose some gift ourselves and then look to the Holy Spirit to impart it; it is not our place to expect the Holy Spirit to impart power to us for a field of service that we have chosen, not he. Rather, it is our place to recognize the divinity and sovereignty of the Spirit and put ourselves unreservedly at his disposal, to let him choose the gift that he wills and impart that to us, and to let him choose the field he wants us in and impart the power that will equip us for it.

I once knew a child of God who, hearing of the baptism with the Holy Spirit and the power that resulted from it, gave up the secular work he had been engaged in at great personal sacrifice. He undertook the work of an evangelist, but the expected power for evangelism did not follow. The man fell into great doubt and darkness until he was led to see that the Holy Spirit *"apportions to each one individually as he wills."* Then, giving up choosing his own field and gifts, he put himself at the Holy Spirit's disposal and let him choose. In the end the Holy Spirit did impart power to this man as an evangelist and a preacher of the word. So we must surrender ourselves completely to the Holy Spirit to work as he wills.

But while the power that the baptism with the Holy Spirit brings will manifest itself in different ways in different individuals, there will always be power. Just as surely as a man is baptized with the Holy Spirit there will be a new power that is not his own—the power of the Highest! Religious biographies abound with instances of men who have worked as best they could until one day they were led to see that there was such an experience as the baptism with the Holy Spirit, and they sought it and obtained it. From that hour a new power filled their ministry that utterly transformed its character. Finney, Brainerd and Moody are cases in point.

But cases of this kind are not confined to a few exceptional men—they are becoming common. I have personally met and corresponded with hundreds during the past twelve months who could testify to the new power that God granted them through the baptism with the Holy Spirit. These hundreds of men and women were in all branches of Christian service. Many of them were ministers of the gospel, others mission workers, others Y.M.C.A. secretaries, others Sunday school teachers, others informal evangelists, others fathers and mothers. Nothing could exceed the clearness, confidence and joyfulness of many of these testimonies. Many have what Christ promised us, and *all* can have it in joyful experience. *"But you will receive power when the Holy Spirit has come upon you."*[15]

To sum up the contents of this chapter, the baptism with the Holy Spirit is the Spirit of God coming upon the believer, taking possession of his faculties, and imparting gifts to him that are not naturally his own but which qualify him for the service God has called him to.

---

[1] *Luke 24:49*
[2] *Acts 19:2*
[3] *Acts 19:6*
[4] *see James 1:18; 1 Peter 1:23*
[5] *e.g. Acts 1:5, 8; 2:4; 4:31, 33*
[6] *Ephesians 3:16-19*
[7] *Romans 8:2*
[8] *Romans 8:13*
[9] *Galatians 5:16*
[10] *e.g. Acts 2:44-46; 4:31-35*
[11] *1 Corinthians 12:30*
[12] *Ephesians 6:4*
[13] *1 Corinthians 12:11*
[14] *1 Corinthians 12:31*
[15] *Acts 1:8*

CHAPTER 2

THE NECESSITY AND OPPORTUNITY

Shortly before Christ was received up into heaven, having committed the preaching of the gospel into his disciples' hands, he laid this very solemn charge upon them concerning the beginning of this great work: *"And behold, I am sending the promise of my Father upon you. But stay in the city until you are clothed with power from on high."*[1]

There is no doubt about what Jesus meant by *"the promise of the Father"* which they were to wait for before beginning the ministry he had entrusted to them. In Acts 1:4-5, we read that Jesus *"ordered them not to depart from Jerusalem, but to wait for the promise of the Father, which, he said, 'you heard from me; for John baptized with water, but you will be baptized with the Holy Spirit not many days from now.'"* The promise of the Father, through which the clothing of power was to come, was the baptism with the Holy Spirit.[2]

Christ then strictly charged his disciples not to presume to take on the work to which he had called them until they had received the baptism with the Holy Spirit—the necessary and all-essential preparation for that work. Jesus said this to men who seemed to have already received very thorough preparation for the work at hand. They had been taught by Christ himself for more than three years. They had heard from his own lips the great truths that they were to proclaim to the world. They had been eyewitnesses of his miracles, of his death and of his resurrection and were about to be eyewitnesses of his ascension. The work before them was simply to go forth and proclaim what their own eyes had seen and what their own ears had heard from the lips of Christ himself.

Weren't they fully prepared for this work? It would seem that way to us. But Christ said, "No. You are so utterly unprepared that you must not take a single step yet. There is a further preparation, so all-essential for effective service that you must wait in Jerusalem until you receive it. This further preparation is the baptism with the Holy Spirit. When you receive that, and not until then, you will be prepared to begin the work I have called you to."

Though these men had received such a unique and unparalleled education for the work he had definitely and clearly called them to, Christ did not permit them to begin that work without receiving the baptism with the Holy Spirit in addition to all that. So how can we undertake the work he has called us to until we have received it in addition to any amount of schooling we may have had for the work? Isn't that a most daring arrogance?

But this is not all. In Acts 10:38, we read *"how God anointed Jesus of Nazareth with the Holy Spirit and with power. He went about doing good and healing all who were oppressed by the devil, for God was with him."* When we look into the Gospels for an explanation of these words, we find it in Luke 3:21-22, 4:14-15, 18, and 21.

We find that at the baptism of Jesus at the Jordan, as he prayed, the Holy Spirit came upon him. Then, *"full of the Holy*

Spirit," he has the temptation experience. Then, *"in the power of the Spirit,"* he begins his ministry, and proclaims that he is anointed to preach because *"the Spirit of the Lord is upon me."* In other words, Jesus Christ never entered into the ministry for which he came into this world until he was baptized with the Holy Spirit.

Jesus Christ had been supernaturally conceived through the Holy Spirit's power; he was the only begotten Son of God; he was divine, very God of very God and yet truly man. If he, *"leaving an example, so that you might follow in his steps,"*[3] did not venture into the ministry for which the Father had sent him until he was baptized with the Holy Spirit, how can we dare to do it? If we dare to do it in the light of these recorded facts, it seems like an offense going beyond arrogance. No doubt it has been done in ignorance by many, but can we plead ignorance any longer?

The baptism with the Holy Spirit is an absolutely necessary preparation for every kind of service for Christ. We may have a very clear call to service, even as clear as the apostles had; but the charge is laid upon us, as it was upon them, that before we begin that service we must wait *"until you are clothed with power from on high."* This clothing with power is through the baptism with the Holy Spirit.

Surely there are few mistakes that we are making today greater than sending men to teach Sunday school classes, engage in evangelism and even preach the gospel, simply because they have been converted and received a certain amount of education—perhaps even college and seminary—but have not yet been baptized with the Holy Spirit. Any man who is in Christian work and has not received the baptism with the Holy Spirit should stop his work right where he is, and not go on with it until he has been *"clothed with power from on high."*

But what will our work do while we are waiting? What did the world do those ten days while the early disciples were waiting? They alone knew the saving truth, yet in obedience to the Lord's command, they were silent. The world was no loser. When the power came they accomplished more in one day than they would have accomplished in years if they had gone on in arrogant disobedience to Christ's charge. We also, after we have received the baptism with the Holy Spirit, will accomplish more in one day than we ever would in years without his power. Days spent in waiting, if it was necessary, would be well spent, but later we will see that there is no need to spend days in waiting.

It may be said that the apostles had gone out on missionary tours during Christ's lifetime, before they were baptized with the Holy Spirit. This is true, but that was before the Holy Spirit was given, and before the command, *"stay in the city until you are clothed with power from on high,"* was given. After that it would have been disobedience and arrogance to have gone out without this clothing with power, and today we are living after the Holy Spirit and the charge to *"wait until clothed"* have been given.

Now we come to the question of the possibility of the baptism with the Holy Spirit. Is the baptism with the Holy Spirit for us?

This question has a most plain and explicit answer in the word of God.

In Acts 2:39, we read, *"For the promise is for you and for your children and for all who are far off, everyone whom the Lord our God calls to himself."* What is *"the promise"* in this passage? Turning back to Acts 1:4-5, we read, *"wait for the promise of the Father, which, he said, 'you heard from me; for John baptized with water, but you will be baptized with the Holy Spirit not many days from now."* Again in Acts 2:33, we read, *"having received from the Father the promise of the Holy Spirit..."*.

It seems perfectly clear that *"the promise"* of Acts 2:39 must be the same as *"the promise"* of Acts 2:33 and of Acts 1:4-5—the promise of the baptism with the Holy Spirit. This conclusion is made absolutely certain by the context: *"Repent and be baptized every one of you in the name of Jesus Christ for the forgiveness of your sins, and you will receive the gift of the Holy Spirit. For the promise is for you..."* etc. So the promise of this verse is the promise of the baptism with the Holy Spirit.

Who is this gift for? Peter says to the Jews whom he was immediately addressing, *"For the promise is for you,"* then looking over their heads to the next generation, *"and for your children."* Then looking down all the coming ages of the Church's history to Gentiles as well as Jews, *"and for all who are far off, everyone whom the Lord our God calls to himself."*

The baptism with the Holy Spirit is for every child of God in every age of the Church's history. If we do not possess this as a personal experience, it is because we have not taken (the exact force of the word *"receive"* in verse 38 is *take*) what God has provided for us in our exalted Savior.[4]

A minister of the gospel once came to me after a lecture on the baptism with the Holy Spirit and said, "The church I belong to teaches that the baptism with the Holy Spirit was for the apostolic age alone."

"It doesn't matter what the church you belong to teaches, or what the church I belong to teaches," I replied. "What does the word of God say?"

Acts 2:39 was read: *"For the promise is for you and for your children and for all who are far off, everyone whom the Lord our God calls to himself."*

"Has he called you?" I asked.

"Yes, he certainly has."

"Is the promise for you?"

"Yes, it is."

And it was. And it is for every child of God who reads these pages.

What a thrilling thought that the baptism with the Holy Spirit, the clothing with power from on high is for us—is for me personally! But that unspeakably joyous thought has a solemn side. If I *can* be baptized with the Holy Spirit, then I *must* be. If I am baptized with the Holy Spirit, then souls will be saved through my instrumentality who will not be saved if I am not baptized with the Holy Spirit. So if I am not willing to pay the price of this baptism and therefore do not receive it, I am responsible before God for all the souls that might have been saved through me, but were not because I was not baptized with the Holy Spirit.

I often tremble for my brothers in Christian work and for myself. It is not because we are teaching deadly error to men; some are guilty of even that, but I am not referring to that now. It is not that we are not teaching the full truth as it is in Jesus. It must be admitted that there are many who do not teach complete error who do not preach a full gospel either, but I am not referring to that now. I tremble for those who are preaching the truth—the truth as it is in Jesus, the gospel in its simplicity, its purity and its fullness—but are preaching it *"in plausible words of wisdom"* and not *"in demonstration of the Spirit and of power"*;[5] preaching it in the energy of the flesh and not in the power of the Holy Spirit.

There is nothing more deadly than the gospel without the Spirit's power. *"For the letter kills, but the Spirit gives life."*[6] It is terribly serious business preaching the gospel either from the pulpit or in more quiet ways. It means death or life to those who hear, and whether it means death or life depends very largely on whether we preach it with or without the baptism with the Holy Spirit. We *must* be baptized with the Holy Spirit.

It is sometimes argued that the baptism with the Holy Spirit was for the purpose of imparting miracle-working power and was for the apostolic age alone. In favor of this position it is argued that the baptism with the Holy Spirit was followed consistently by miracles. The unreasonableness of this position is seen, firstly, by the fact that Christ himself claimed that the purpose of the baptism with the Holy Spirit was to impart power for *witnessing*, and not specific power for working miracles.[7] Secondly, Paul distinctly taught that there were diversities of gifts, and that *"working of miracles"* was only one of the varied manifestations of the baptism with the Holy Spirit.[8] Lastly, Peter distinctly says in Acts 2:38-39 that the gift of the Holy Spirit (*"the promise"*) is for all believers in all generations. It is clear from comparing Acts 2:39 with Luke 24:49, Acts 1:4-5, 2:33 and 2:38, and by comparing Acts 10:45 with Acts 11:15-16, that both of these expressions of *"the promise"* and *"the gift of the Holy Spirit,"* refer to the baptism with the Holy Spirit.

If we take miracles in the broad sense of all results brought about by supernatural power, then it is true that each one baptized with the Holy Spirit does receive miracle-working power, for everyone who is baptized in this way receives a power that is not their own, but God's own supernatural power. But the result of the baptism with the Holy Spirit that was most noticeable and essential was power to convince, convict and convert.[9] There seem to have been no displays of miracle-working power immediately following Paul's baptism with the Holy Spirit, even though he became so remarkably gifted in this way later. What he received in immediate connection with the baptism with the Holy Spirit was power to witness for Jesus as the Son of God.

---

[1] *Luke 24:49*
[2] *see Acts 1:8*
[3] *1 Peter 2:21*
[4] *see Acts 2:33; John 7:38-39*
[5] *1 Corinthians 2:4*
[6] *2 Corinthians 3:6*
[7] *see Acts 1:5, 8; Luke 24:48-49*
[8] *1 Corinthians 12:4, 8-11*
[9] *Acts 2:4, 37, 41; 4:8-13, 31, 33; 9:17, 20-22*

CHAPTER 3

HOW TO OBTAIN IT

We have now come to a place where there is a deep sense that we must be baptized with the Holy Spirit. The practical question confronts us: how can we obtain this baptism with the Holy Spirit which we so desperately need? The word of God also answers this question very plainly and specifically.

The Bible points out a path consisting of seven simple steps. Anyone who wants to can take this path, and whoever takes these seven steps will, with absolute certainty, enter into this blessing. This statement may seem very confident, but the word of God is equally confident regarding the outcome of taking these steps which it points out. All seven steps are stated or implied in Acts 2:38: *"Repent and be baptized every one of you in the name of Jesus Christ for the forgiveness of your sins, and you will receive the gift of the Holy Spirit."* The first three steps in particular are clearly brought out in this verse, and the others which are clearly implied in the verse are better brought out by other passages which we will refer to later.

The first step is found in the word "repent". What does "repent" mean? To change your mind. Change your mind about what? About God, about Christ, and about sin. In any given case, what this change of mind is about must be determined by the context. Here the first and most prominent thought is a change of mind about Christ.

Peter has just brought a terrible charge against his hearers—that they had crucified the one whom God had made both Lord and Christ. Cut to the heart by this charge which had been carried home by the power of the Holy Spirit, his hearers cried out, *"Brothers, what shall we do?"* *"Repent,"* Peter answered. Change your mind about Christ. Change from a Christ-hating and Christ-crucifying attitude of mind to a Christ-accepting attitude of mind. Accept Jesus as Christ and Lord.

So this is the first step toward the baptism with the Holy Spirit: Accept Jesus as Christ and Lord.

The second step is also found in the word "repent." While the change of mind about Jesus is the first and prominent thought, there must also be a change of mind about sin; a change of mind from a sin-loving or sin-indulging attitude of mind to a sin-hating and sin-renouncing attitude of mind. So the second step is to renounce sin—all sin, every sin.

Here we come to one of the most common obstacles to receiving the Holy Spirit—sin. Something is held on to in our inmost hearts that we more or less clearly feel is not pleasing to God. If we are to receive the Holy Spirit, there must be very honest and very thorough heart searching. We cannot do satisfactory searching ourselves—God must do it. If we want to receive the

Holy Spirit, we should go alone with God and ask him to thoroughly search us and bring to light anything that displeases him,[1] then wait for him to do it. When the displeasing thing is revealed it should be done away with immediately. If nothing is brought to light after patient and honest waiting, we can conclude that there is nothing of this kind in the way and go on to the further steps. But we should not conclude this too quickly. The sin that hinders the blessing may be something that appears very small and insignificant in itself.

Mr. Finney tells of a young woman who was deeply concerned about obtaining the baptism with the Holy Spirit. Night after night she agonized in prayer, but the desired blessing did not come. One night as she was in prayer, a matter of head adornment came up before her that had troubled her before. Putting her hand to her head, she took the pins out and threw them away and immediately the blessing came.

This was a small matter in itself, a matter that would not have appeared to many as sin, but it was a matter of controversy between this woman and God. When this was settled the blessing came. *"For whatever does not proceed from faith is sin,"*[2] and it doesn't matter how little the thing may be—if there are questions about it, it must be done away with if we are to have the baptism with the Holy Spirit.

So the second step toward the baptism with the Holy Spirit is to put away every sin.

The third step is found in this same verse: *"Be baptized every one of you for the forgiveness of your sins."* It was immediately after Jesus' baptism that the Holy Spirit descended upon him.[3] Though he was sinless, Jesus humbled himself in baptism to take the sinner's place, and then God highly exalted him by giving the Holy Spirit and by the audible testimony, *"You are my beloved Son; with you I am well pleased."* So we must humble ourselves by openly confessing our sins and renouncing them, as well as openly confessing our acceptance of Christ Jesus in God's appointed way—baptism.

The baptism with the Holy Spirit is not for the one who secretly takes his place as a sinner and believer in Christ, but for the one who does so openly. Of course, the baptism with the Holy Spirit can happen before water baptism, as in the case of the household of Cornelius.[4] But this was obviously an exceptional case, and water baptism immediately followed. I have little doubt that there have been those among Christians who did not believe in or practice water baptism—for example, "the Friends" or "Quakers"—who have received and given evidence of the baptism with the Holy Spirit, but the passage before us certainly presents the normal order.

The fourth step is clearly implied in the verse we have been studying (Acts 2:38), but it is brought out more clearly in Acts 5:32: *"God has given* [the Holy Spirit] *to those who obey him."* The fourth step is obedience.

What does obedience mean? It does not mean merely doing some of the things, many of the things or most of the things that God calls us to do. It means total surrender to the will of God. Obedience is the attitude of the will that lies behind the actual acts of obedience. It means that I come to God and say, "Heavenly Father, here I am, and here is everything I have. You have bought me with a price, and I acknowledge your complete ownership. Take me and all I have, and do with me whatever you want. Send me where you want, use me as you want. I surrender myself and all I possess completely, unconditionally and forever to your control and use."

It was when the burnt offering was laid upon the altar whole, with no part held back, that *"fire came out from before the LORD,"*[5] and accepted the gift. And it is when we bring ourselves as a whole burnt offering to the Lord, and lay ourselves upon the altar, that the fire comes and God accepts the gift.

Here we touch on the barrier to receiving the baptism with the Holy Spirit for many people: there is not total surrender. The will is not laid down, the heart does not cry, "Lord, where you want, what you want, as you want it!" One man desires the baptism with the Holy Spirit so that he can preach or work with power in Boston, when God actually wants him in Bombay. Another wants it so that he can preach to popular audiences, when God wants him to labor among the poor.

A young woman at a convention had a strong desire to hear someone speak on the baptism with the Holy Spirit, and the sermon went home with power to her heart. For some time she had been in deep agony of soul when I asked her what it was that she desired. "Oh," she cried, "I can't go back to Baltimore until I'm baptized with the Holy Spirit."

"Is your will laid down?"

"I don't know."

"Do you desire to go back to Baltimore to be a Christian worker?"

"Yes."

"Are you willing to go back to Baltimore and be a servant girl if that is where God wants you?"

"No, I'm not."

"Well, you will never get the baptism with the Holy Spirit until you are. Will you lay your will down?"

"I can't."

"Are you willing to let God lay it down for you?"

"Yes."

"Well then, ask him to do it."

She bowed her head in brief but sincere prayer.

"Did God hear that prayer?"

"He must have, it was according to his will ... he did."

"Now ask him for the baptism with the Holy Spirit."

Again she bowed her head, and the brief, sincere prayer ascended to God. There was a brief silence and the agony was over—the blessing had come when the will was surrendered.

There are many who hold back from this total surrender because they fear God's will. They are afraid that God's will may be something dreadful. But remember who God is—he is our Father. Never has an earthly father had such loving and tender desires regarding his children as he has toward us. *"No good thing does he withhold from those who walk uprightly."*[6] *"He who did not spare his own Son but gave him up for us all, how will he not also with him graciously give us all things?"*[7]

There is nothing to be feared in God's will; it will always ultimately prove to be the best and sweetest thing in all his universe.

The fifth step is found in Luke 11:13: *"If you then, who are evil, know how to give good gifts to your children, how much more will the heavenly Father give the Holy Spirit to those who ask him!"*

The asking of this verse is the asking that springs from real and intense desire. This is brought out by the context: *"And I tell you, ask, and it will be given to you; seek, and you will find; knock, and it will be opened to you."* Also note the parable of the persistent friend that comes immediately before this. Clearly the asking that Christ has in mind is not the asking of a passing and half-hearted whim, but the asking of intense desire.

There is a very suggestive passage in Isaiah 44:3: *"For I will pour water on the thirsty land, and streams on the dry ground; I will pour my Spirit upon your offspring, and my blessing on your descendants."* What does it mean to be thirsty? When a person is thirsty there is only one cry: "Water! Water! Water!" Every pore in their body seems to have a voice and cry out "Water!" So when our hearts have one cry, "The Holy Spirit! The Holy Spirit! The Holy Spirit!" then God pours floods upon the dry ground, pours his Spirit upon us. So this is the fifth step: intense desire for the baptism with the Holy Spirit. On that day when Pentecost had fully come, the thirsty souls of the early disciples were filled, even to the extent of their longing that had been brought by ten days of eager waiting.

As long as a person thinks he can somehow get along without the baptism with the Holy Spirit, as long as he continues searching around for the right education or cunningly concocted methods of work, he is not going to receive it. There are many ministers who are missing the fullness of power God has for them simply because they are not willing to admit the lack there has been all these years of their ministry. It is certainly humiliating to confess this, but that humiliating confession would be the precursor of a marvelous blessing.

But there are many who, in their unwillingness to make this healthy confession, are searching around for some ingenious method of exegesis to get around the plain and simple meaning of God's word. They are cheating themselves out of the fullness of the Spirit's power that God is so eager to give them, not to mention jeopardizing the eternal welfare of the souls that are dependant upon their ministry, and could be won for Christ if they had the power of the Holy Spirit available to them.

But there are others whom God in his grace has brought to see that there was something their ministry lacked, and that this something was nothing less than that all-essential baptism with the Holy Spirit. They have realized that without this a person is completely unqualified for acceptable and effective service, and have humbly and openly confessed their lack. Sometimes they have been led to the God-taught resolution that they would not go on in their work until this lack was supplied, and they have waited on God the Father in eager longing for the fulfillment of his promise—and the result has been a transformed ministry for which many have risen to bless God.

It is not enough that the desire for the baptism with the Holy Spirit be intense, it must also have the right motive. There is a desire for the baptism with the Holy Spirit that is purely selfish. Many men have an intense desire for the baptism with the Holy Spirit simply so they may be a great preacher, or a great street evangelist, or in some way become a renowned Christian. It is simply their own gain or glory that they are seeking. It is ultimately not the Holy Spirit that they seek, but their own honor, and the baptism with the Holy Spirit is simply a means to that end.

One of the subtlest and most dangerous snares into which Satan leads us is to seek the Holy Spirit, the most sacred of all gifts, for our own ends. The desire for the Holy Spirit must not be in order to make that glorious and divine Person the servant of our low aspirations, but for the glory of God. It must arise from a recognition that God and Christ are being dishonored by my powerless ministry, and by the sin of the people around me against which I now have no power, but that he will be honored if I have the baptism with the Spirit of God.

One of the most serious passages in the New Testament bears upon this point: *"Now when Simon saw that the Spirit was given through the laying on of the apostles' hands, he offered them money, saying, 'Give me this power also, so that anyone on whom I lay my hands may receive the Holy Spirit.'"*[8] There was a strong desire on Simon's part, but it was entirely unholy and selfish, and Peter's dreadful answer is worthy of note and meditation. Aren't there many today who desire the baptism with the Holy Spirit with equally unholy and selfish ambition?

Everyone who is desiring and seeking the baptism with the Holy Spirit would do well to ask himself why he desires it. If you find that it is merely for your own gratification or glory, then ask God to forgive you the thought of your heart and enable you to see how you need it for his glory and to desire it for that reason.

The sixth step is also in Luke 11:13: *"If you then, who are evil, know how to give good gifts to your children, how much more will the heavenly Father give the Holy Spirit to those who ask him!"* The sixth step is to ask—specific asking for a specific blessing.

When Christ has been accepted and confessed as Savior and Master; when sin has been put away; when there has been the definite, total surrender of the will; when there is a real and holy desire, then comes the simple act of asking God for this specific blessing. It is given in answer to sincere, definite, specific, believing prayer.

It has been sincerely disputed by some that we should not pray for the Holy Spirit. They reason it out like this: "The Holy Spirit was given to the Church at Pentecost as a remaining gift." This is true, but each believer must claim for himself what was given to the Church. It is certainly true that God has already given Christ to the world,[9] but each individual must claim him by a personal act to receive the personal benefit of the gift. In the same way each individual must personally claim God's gift of the Holy Spirit to get the personal benefit of it.

But it is argued still further that each believer has the Holy Spirit. This is also true in a sense. *"Anyone who does not have the Spirit of Christ does not belong to him."*[10] But as we have already seen, it is quite possible to have some—even much—of the Spirit's presence and work in our heart and yet come short of that special fullness and work known in the Bible as the baptism or filling with the Holy Spirit. In answer to all false reasonings on this subject we put the simple words of Christ: *"How much more will the heavenly Father give the Holy Spirit to those who ask him!"*

I was announced to speak on this subject at a convention, and a brother said to me, "I see you're going to speak on the baptism with the Holy Spirit."

"Yes."

"It's the most important subject on the program! Now, be sure and tell them not to pray for the Holy Spirit."

"I will certainly not tell them that! Jesus said, *'how much more will the heavenly Father give the Holy Spirit to those who ask him.'*"

"Oh, but that was before Pentecost."

"How about Acts 4:31? Was that before Pentecost or after?"

"After it, of course."

"Well, read it."

It was read: *"And when they had prayed, the place in which they were gathered together was shaken, and they were all filled with the Holy Spirit and continued to speak the word of God with boldness."*

"How about Acts 8? Was that before Pentecost or after?"

"After, of course."

"Well, read Acts 8:14-16."

The verses were read: *"They sent to them Peter and John, who came down and prayed for them that they might receive the Holy Spirit, for he had not yet fallen on any of them...and they received the Holy Spirit."*

Against all assumptions, this teaching of the word is clear by precept and example: the Holy Spirit is given in answer to prayer. It was so at Pentecost, and it has been so since. Those whom I have met who give most evidence of the Spirit's presence and power in their life and work believe in praying for the Holy Spirit. It has been my unspeakable privilege to pray with many ministers and Christian workers for this great blessing, and afterward to learn from them or from others of the new power that has come into their service—none other than the power of the Holy Spirit.

The seventh and last step is found in Mark 11:24: *"Therefore I tell you, whatever you ask in prayer, believe that you have received it, and it will be yours."*

Even God's most definite and unconditional promises must be claimed by faith. In James 1:5 we read, *"If any of you lacks wisdom, let him ask God, who gives generously to all without reproach, and it will be given him."* Now, that is certainly definite and unconditional enough, but listen to what the writer says next: *"But let him ask in faith, with no doubting, for the one who doubts is like a wave of the sea that is driven and tossed by the wind. For that person must not suppose that he will receive anything from the Lord."* So there must be faith in order to make even the most definite and unconditional promises of God our own, like the ones in Luke 11:13 and Acts 2:38-39.

Here we discover the cause of failure in many cases to enter into the blessing of the baptism with the Holy Spirit. The failure is because the last step is not taken—the simple step of faith. They do not believe, they do not confidently expect, and we have another instance of how men failed to enter because of unbelief.[11] There are many, very many, who are kept out of this land of milk and honey just by this unbelief.

There is a faith that goes beyond expectation—a faith that just puts out its hand and takes what it asks. I remember how greatly confused I was by Mark 11:24 when I first noticed it. On examining the Greek of the passage I saw that the translation was correct, but what did it mean? It seemed like the tenses were confused: *"Believe that you have* [already] *received it, and it will be yours."* This apparent enigma was solved long after, while I was studying the first letter of John. I read 1 John 5:14-15: *"And this is the confidence that we have toward him, that if we ask anything according to his will he hears us. And if we know that he hears us in whatever we ask, we know that we have the requests that we have asked of him."*

When I ask anything of God, the first thing to find out is if it is according to his will. When that is settled and I find that it is according to his will (for example, when what I am asking for is clearly promised in his word), then I know the prayer is heard. And I know further that I have the requests that I have asked of him. I know this because he plainly says so, and what I have claimed in simple, childlike faith in his naked word I will have in actual experience.

When someone who has a clear title to a piece of property deeds it to me it is mine as soon as the deed is properly executed and recorded, though it may be some time before I actually get to enjoy it. I have it in one sense as soon as the deed is recorded, and I will have it in the other sense later. In the same way, as soon as we have met the conditions of successful prayer and ask God for *"anything according to his will,"* it is our privilege to know that the prayer is heard, and that what we have asked of him is ours.

Now apply this to the baptism with the Holy Spirit. I have met the conditions of obtaining this blessing, which have already been mentioned. I simply, specifically ask God the Father for the baptism with the Holy Spirit. Then I stop and ask if that prayer was according to his will. It is—Luke 11:13 says so. *"If you then, who are evil, know how to give good gifts to your children, how much more will the heavenly Father give the Holy Spirit to those who ask him!"* Acts 2:38-39 says, *"Repent and be baptized every one of you in the name of Jesus Christ for the forgiveness of your sins, and you will receive the gift of the Holy Spirit. For the promise is for you and for your children and for all who are far off, everyone whom the Lord our God calls to himself."*

It is clear that the prayer for the baptism with the Holy Spirit is according to his will, because it is specifically and plainly promised. So I know that the prayer is heard and that I have the request I have asked of him—I have the baptism with the Holy Spirit.[12] I then have the right to rise from my knees and say, on the all-sufficient authority of God's word, "I have the baptism with the Holy Spirit," and afterwards I will enjoy in actual experience what I have claimed by simple faith—for God has said it and he cannot lie, *"whatever you ask in prayer, believe that you have received it, and it will be yours."*

If any reader of this book has accepted Christ as Savior and Lord and confessed it in God's way; if they have searched out sin and done away with it; if they have totally surrendered their will and self to God; if they have a true desire to be baptized with the Holy Spirit for God's glory—if these conditions have been met, you can put this book down, kneel right now before God and ask him to baptize you with the Holy Spirit. And when the prayer has gone up, you can then say, "That prayer was heard and I have what I've asked for—I have the baptism with the Holy Spirit." You have the right to get up and go out to your work, assured that in that work you will have the Holy Spirit's power.

But someone will ask, "Don't I need to know that I have the baptism with the Holy Spirit before I begin the work?" Of course! But how will we know? I know of no better way of knowing anything than by God's word. I would believe God's word before my feelings any day. How do we deal with an inquirer who has accepted Christ but lacks assurance that he has eternal life? We do not ask him to look at his feelings, but rather we take him to some passage like John 3:36. We tell him to read it and he reads, *"Whoever believes in the Son has eternal life; whoever does not obey the Son shall not see life, but the wrath of God remains on him."*

"Do you believe in the Son?"

"Yes."

"What do you have, then?"

"Oh, I don't know—I don't feel that I have eternal life yet."

"But what does *God* say?"

"Whoever believes in the Son has eternal life."

"Are you going to believe God or your feelings?"

We hold the inquirer right there until on the simple, naked word of God, feelings or no feelings, he says, "I know I have eternal life because God says so," and afterwards the feeling comes. Deal with yourself in just the same way in this matter of the baptism with the Holy Spirit. Be sure you have met the conditions, and then simply ask, claim, and act.

But someone will say, "Will it be just as it was before? Won't there be any manifestation?" Most assuredly there will be some manifestation. *"To each is given the manifestation of the Spirit for the common good."*[13] What kind of manifestation will it be? Where will we see it? It is at this point that many make a mistake. They have, perhaps, read the life of Mr. Finney or of Jonathan Edwards, and recall how great waves of electric emotion swept over these men until they were forced to ask God to withdraw his hand for fear that they would die from the ecstasy. Or they have gone to some meeting and heard testimonies of similar experiences, and they expect something like this.

Now I do not deny the reality of such experiences—I cannot. The testimony of men like Finney and Edwards should be believed. There is a stronger reason why I cannot deny them. But while admitting the reality of these experiences, I would ask, where is there a single line of the New Testament that describes any such experience in connection with the baptism with the Holy Spirit? Every manifestation of the baptism with the Holy Spirit in the New Testament was for new power in service.

For example, look at 1 Corinthians 12, where this subject is treated very thoroughly. Note the kind of manifestations mentioned. It is quite probable that the apostles had similar experiences to those of Finney and Edwards and others, but if they had, the Holy Spirit kept them from recording them. It is good that he did, because if they had told about it we would have looked for these things rather than the more important manifestation of power in service.

But another question will be asked, "Didn't the apostles wait ten days? So is it possible that we have to wait?" The apostles were kept waiting ten days, but the reason is given in Acts 2:1: *"When the day of Pentecost arrived..."* (literally "was being fulfilled"). In the eternal purposes and plans of God and in the Old Testament foreshadowing, the day of Pentecost was set as the time for the giving of the Holy Spirit, and the Spirit could not be given until the day of Pentecost was fulfilled—but we read of no waiting after Pentecost.

In Acts 4:31, there was no waiting. *"And when they had prayed, the place in which they were gathered together was shaken, and they were all filled with the Holy Spirit and continued to speak the word of God with boldness."* In Acts 8 there was no waiting. When Peter and John came down to Samaria and found that none of the young converts had been baptized with the Holy Spirit, they *"prayed for them that they might receive the Holy Spirit,"* and they did then and there.[14] Paul of Tarsus was not forced to wait in Acts 9. Ananias came in and told him of this wondrous gift, baptized him, and laid his hands upon him, and *"immediately he proclaimed Jesus in the synagogues, saying, 'He is the Son of God.'"*[15] There was no waiting in Acts 10. Before Peter had finished his sermon the baptism with the Holy Spirit came.[16] In Acts 19 there was no waiting. As soon as Paul had declared the gift of the Holy Spirit to the Ephesian disciples and the conditions were met, the blessing followed.[17]

Men only have to wait when they do not meet the conditions—when Christ is not accepted, or sin is not put away, or there is not total surrender, or true desire, or definite prayer, or simple faith on the naked word of God. The absence of some of these things keeps many waiting for sometimes more than ten days, but there is no need for any reader of this book to wait ten hours. You can have the baptism with the Holy Spirit right now if you want to.

A young man once came to me in great sincerity about this matter. "I heard of the baptism with the Holy Spirit some time ago," he said, "and I've been seeking it, but I haven't received it."

"Is your will laid down?"

"I'm afraid that's the trouble."

"Will you lay it down?"

"I'm afraid I can't."

"Are you willing to let God lay it down for you?"

"Yes."

"Ask him to."

We knelt in prayer, and he asked God to lay down his will for him.

"Did God hear that?" I asked him.

"He must have, it was according to his will."

"Is your will laid down?"

"It must be."

"Then ask God for the baptism with the Holy Spirit."

He did this.

"Was that prayer according to his will?"

"Yes."

"Was it heard?"

"It must have been."

"Do you have the baptism with the Holy Spirit?"

"I don't feel it."

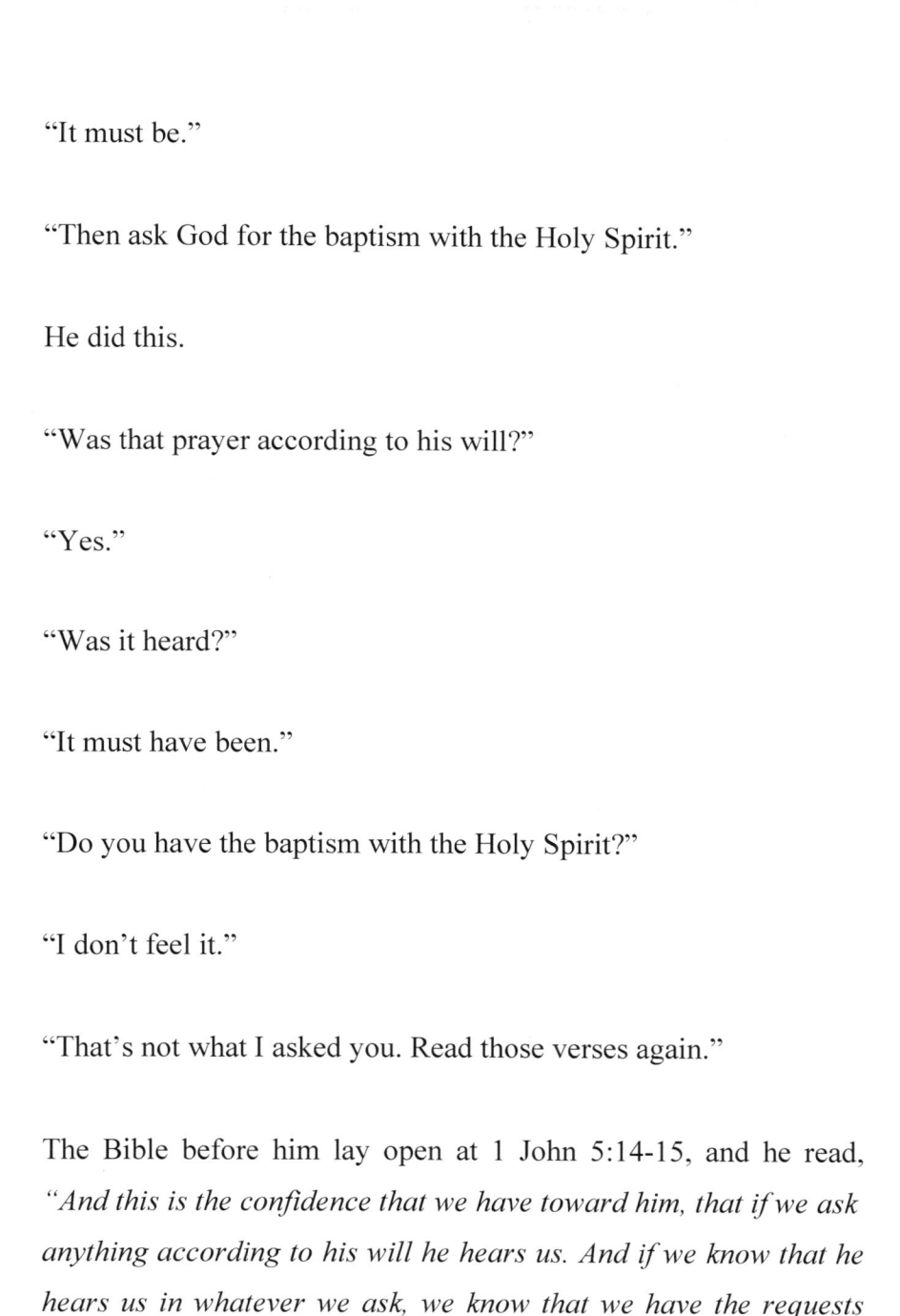

"That's not what I asked you. Read those verses again."

The Bible before him lay open at 1 John 5:14-15, and he read, *"And this is the confidence that we have toward him, that if we ask anything according to his will he hears us. And if we know that he hears us in whatever we ask, we know that we have the requests that we have asked of him."*

"What was the request?"

"The baptism with the Holy Spirit."

"Do you have it?"

"I don't feel it, but God says so, so I must have it."

A few days later I met him again and asked if he really had received what he took on simple faith. With a happy look on his face he answered, "Yes."

I lost sight of him for perhaps two years, and then found him preparing for the ministry. He was already preaching, and God was honoring his preaching with souls being saved. A little later he used him along with others to greatly bless the theological seminary where he was studying. He also decided to serve Christ in the foreign field. What he claimed and received on simple faith, any reader of this book can claim and receive in the same way.

---

[1] *Psalm 139:23-24*

[2] *Romans 14:23*

[3] *Luke 3:21-22*

[4] *Acts 10:44-48*

[5] *Leviticus 9:24*

[6] *Psalm 84:11*

[7] *Romans 8:32*

[8] *Acts 8:18-24*
[9] *John 3:16*
[10] *Romans 8:9*
[11] *Hebrews 3:19*
[12] *1 John 5:14-15*
[13] *1 Corinthians 12:7*
[14] *Acts 8:15, 17*
[15] *Acts 9:17, 20*
[16] *compare Acts 10:44-46 and Acts 11:15-16*
[17] *Acts 19:1-6*

CHAPTER 4

REFILLED WITH THE SPIRIT

In Acts 2:4, we read: *"And they were all filled with the Holy Spirit and began to speak in other tongues as the Spirit gave them utterance."* This was the fulfillment of Acts 1:5, *"You will be baptized with the Holy Spirit not many days from now."*

Peter was one of those mentioned by name as being *"filled with the Holy Spirit,"* or *"baptized with the Holy Spirit."* In Acts 4:8, we read, *"Then Peter, filled with the Holy Spirit, said to them..."* etc. Here Peter experienced a new filling with the Holy Spirit. Again, in Acts 4:31, we read, *"And when they had prayed, the place in which they were gathered together was shaken, and they were all filled with the Holy Spirit and continued to speak the word of God with boldness."* Peter is named as one of this group,[1] so we see that here Peter experienced a third filling with the Holy Spirit.

It is clear that it is not sufficient to be baptized with the Holy Spirit merely once. As new emergencies of service arise, there must be new fillings with the Spirit. The failure to realize this has led to very sad and serious results in the ministries of many. They have been baptized with the Holy Spirit at some period in their life, and strive to get through their whole future life in the power of this past experience. It is largely for this reason that we see so many men who once unquestionably worked in the Holy Spirit's power who give little evidence of the possession of that power today.

For each new service that is to be conducted, for each new soul that is to be dealt with, for each new service for Christ that is to be performed, for each new day and each new emergency of Christian life and service, we should definitely seek a new filling with the Holy Spirit. I do not deny that there is an *"anointing that abides,"*[2] nor do I deny the permanency of the gifts that the Holy Spirit gives; I simply stress with clear and abundant Scriptural proof—to say nothing of proof from experience and observation—that this gift must not be neglected,[3] but rather fanned into flame.[4] Repeated fillings with the Holy Spirit are necessary to continue and increase in power.

Now the question arises: should these new fillings with the Holy Spirit be called fresh baptisms with the Holy Spirit? On the one hand, it must be admitted that in Acts 2:4, the expression *"filled with the Holy Spirit"* is used to describe the experience promised in Acts 1:5 (*"You will be baptized with the Holy Spirit"*), so these two expressions are synonymous to this extent. On the other hand, however, it should be noticed that the expression "baptized with the Holy Spirit" is used nowhere in the Bible of any experience but the first. Furthermore, the word "baptized" itself suggests an initial or initiatory experience.

So while we stand for the truth that those who speak of "fresh baptisms with the Holy Spirit" are aiming at, it would seem wisest to follow the uniform usage of the Bible and speak of the experiences that succeed the first as being "filled with the Holy Spirit," and not as being "baptized with the Holy Spirit."

---

[1] *Acts 4:19, 23*
[2] *1 John 2:27*
[3] *1 Timothy 4:14*
[4] *2 Timothy 1:6*

CHAPTER 5

HOW SPIRITUAL POWER IS LOST

Any discussion of the baptism with the Holy Spirit and the power which comes from it would be incomplete if we did not call attention to the fact that spiritual power can be lost.

One of the strangest and saddest stories of Old Testament history is that of Samson. It is also one of the most instructive. He was by far the most remarkable man of his day; the grandest opportunities were open to him. But after striking temporary victories, his life ended in tragic failure, all through his own inexcusable foolishness.

Time and again it is said of him that the Spirit of the Lord came upon him mightily, and in the power of that Spirit he was able to do things that astonished his own people and humiliated the enemies of the Lord. But in Judges 16:19-20, we see the Lord desert him. Though he was unconscious of it, his strength had gone and he was about to be taken into wretched captivity, the joke of the godless. He would ultimately die with the enemies of the Lord in a violent and dishonored death.

Unfortunately, Samson is not the only man in Christian history who, having once known the power of the Holy Spirit, has afterward been shorn of this power and laid aside. There have been many Samsons, and I presume there will be many more—men whom God has once used and has afterward been forced to lay aside. Such a man is one of the saddest sights on earth. Let us look at when the Lord departs from a man or withdraws his power from him—in other words, how power is lost.

First of all, God withdraws his power from men when they go back on their separation to him.

This was the precise case with Samson himself.[1] His uncut hair was the outward sign of his Nazirite vow, by which he separated himself to the Lord. The shaving of his hair was the surrender of his separation, and when his separation was given up his strength was lost.

It is at this same point that many men today lose their power. There was a day when they separated themselves to God; they turned their back completely upon the world and its ambitions, its spirit, its purposes. They set themselves apart to God as holy to him and to be his, for God to take them and use them and do with them what he wanted. And God honored their separation and anointed them with the Holy Spirit and power—God has used them.

But Delilah has come to them. The world has captured their hearts again. They have listened to the world's siren voice and allowed her to shave them of the sign of separation. They are no longer separated men, wholly consecrated to the Lord, and the Lord leaves him.

Aren't there such people among those who are reading this? Men and women the Lord once used, but he does not use you now.

You may still be in Christian work outwardly, but there is not the old freedom and power in it. This is the reason: you have been untrue to your separation, to your consecration to God. You are listening to Delilah, to the voice of the harlot—the world and its attractiveness.

Do you want to get the old power back again? There is only one thing to do—let your hair grow again as Samson did. Renew your consecration to God.

Secondly, power is lost through sin.

It was this way with Saul, the son of Kish. The Spirit of God came upon Saul, and he won a great victory for God.[2] He advanced the people of God to a place of triumph over their enemies who had held them under for years. But Saul disobeyed God in two specific instances.[3] The Lord withdrew his favor and his power, and Saul's life ended in utter defeat and ruin. This is the history of many men whom God has once used. Sin has crept in. They have done what God told them not to do, or have refused to do what he told them to do, and the power of God has been withdrawn.

The one who has known God's power in service and wants to continue in it must walk very softly before him. He must be listening constantly to hear what God tells him to do or not do. He must respond quickly to the slightest whisper of God. Undoubtedly anyone who has once known God's power would rather die than lose it, but it is lost when sin comes in.

Are there those who are passing through this dreadful experience of the loss of God's power who are reading this book? Ask yourself if the reason is not this: that sin has crept in somewhere. Are you doing something, some little thing, perhaps, that God tells you not to do? Are you leaving something undone that God tells you to do? Set this matter right with God and the old power will come back. David was guilty of an awful sin, but when that sin was confessed and put away, he came to know the power of the Spirit again.[4]

If we want to continually experience the power of God we must often get alone with him—at the close of each day at least—and ask him to show us if any sin, anything displeasing in his sight, has crept in that day. If he shows us that there is something, we must confess it and put it away then and there.

Thirdly, power is lost through self-indulgence.

The one who wants to have God's power must lead a life of self-denial. There are many things which are not sinful in the ordinary understanding of the word "sin", but which hinder spirituality and rob men of power. I do not believe that any man can lead a life of luxury, overindulge his natural appetites and indulge extensively in delicacies, and enjoy the fullness of God's power. Satisfying the flesh and the fullness of the Spirit do not go hand in hand. *"For the desires of the flesh are against the Spirit, and the desires of the Spirit are against the flesh, for these are opposed to each other."*[5] Paul wrote, *"But I discipline my body and keep it under control."*[6]

We live in a day when the temptation to indulge the flesh is very great. Luxuries are common. Piety and prosperity often go hand in hand, and in many of these cases the prosperity that piety and power have brought has been the ruin of the man to whom it has come. Many ministers of power have become popular and in demand, and with the increasing popularity has come an increase of pay and the comforts of life. Luxurious living has come in, and the power of the Spirit has gone out. It would not be difficult to cite specific instances of this sad truth. If we want to experience the continuing power of the Spirit, we need to be on guard to lead lives of simplicity, free from indulgence and excess, always ready to *"share in suffering as a good soldier of Christ Jesus."*[7]

I openly confess that I am afraid of luxury—not as afraid of it as I am of sin, but it comes next as an object of dread. It is a very subtle but very potent enemy of power. There are devils today that never come out except by prayer and fasting.[8]

Fourthly, power is lost through greed for money.

It was through this that a member of the original apostles fell—one of the twelve whom Jesus himself chose to be with him. The love of money—the love of accumulation—got into the heart of Judas Iscariot, and became his ruin. *"For the love of money is a root of all kinds of evils,"*[9] but one of the greatest evils of which it is the root is the loss of spiritual power.

How many men there are today who once knew what spiritual power was, but money began to come. They soon felt its strange fascination. The love for accumulation, covetousness, the love for more, little by little took possession of them. They have accumulated their money honestly, but it has absorbed them. The Spirit of God is shut out and his power has departed.

Men who want to have power need to have the words of Christ, *"Take care, and be on your guard against all covetousness,"*[10] written large and engraved deeply upon their hearts. A person does not need to be rich to be covetous. A very poor man may be just as much absorbed in the desire for wealth as any greedy millionaire.

Fifthly, power is lost through pride.

This is the subtlest and most dangerous of all the enemies of power. I am confident that more men lose their power at this point than at any of the others mentioned so far. There are many men who have not consciously gone back upon their consecration, have not let sin creep into their lives—in the sense of consciously doing what God has forbidden them to do or consciously refusing to do what he has commanded. They have not given into self-indulgence, and have totally refused the seduction of the accumulation of money with continual persistence. But they have still failed, because pride has come in. They have become puffed up because of the very fact that God has given them power and used them. They may even be puffed up over the consistency and simplicity and devotion of their lives, and God has been forced to set them aside.

God cannot use a proud man. *"God opposes the proud but gives grace to the humble."*[11] The man who is puffed up with pride (which is self-confidence) cannot be filled up with the Holy Spirit. Paul saw this danger for himself. God saw it for him, *"So to keep me from becoming conceited because of the surpassing greatness of the revelations, a thorn was given me in the flesh, a messenger of Satan to harass me, to keep me from becoming conceited."*[12]

How many men have failed here! They have sought God's power—sought it in God's way!—and it has come. Men have testified of the blessing received through their word, and pride has entered and been indulged, and all is lost. Moses was the meekest of men, and yet he failed at this very point: *"Shall we bring water for you out of this rock?"* he cried, and then and there God laid him aside.[13]

If God is using us at all, let us get down very low before him—the more he uses us the lower let us get. May God keep his own words ringing in our ears: *"Clothe yourselves, all of you, with humility toward one another, for 'God opposes the proud but gives grace to the humble.'"*

Sixthly, power is lost through neglect of prayer.

It is especially in prayer that we are charged with the energy of God. It is the man who is much in prayer into whom God's power flows mightily. John Livingston once spent a night with some Christians in a prayer meeting. The next day, June 21st of 1630, he preached at the Kirk of Shotts, and the Spirit so fell upon his hearers that five hundred could either date their conversion or some remarkable confirmation from that day forward. This is but one instance among thousands to show how power is given in prayer.

Power is constantly going from us in service and blessing, just as from Christ.[14] If power is to be maintained, it must be constantly renewed in prayer. When electricity is given off from a charged body it must be recharged. In the same way, we must be recharged with divine energy, and this is done by coming into contact with God in prayer. Many men whom God has used have become lazy in their habits of prayer, and the Lord departs from them and their power is gone. Are there not some of us who do not have the power today that we once had, simply because we do not spend the time on our faces before God that we once did?

Finally, power is lost through neglect of the word of God.

God's power comes through prayer, and it also comes through the word of God.[15] Many have known the power that comes through the regular, thoughtful, prayerful, lengthy meditation upon the word of God. But business and perhaps Christian duties have multiplied, other studies have come in, the word of God has been more or less crowded out, and power has gone.

We must meditate daily, prayerfully, deeply on the word of God if we are to maintain power. Many men have run dry through its neglect.

I think these seven points give the main ways in which spiritual power is lost—I can think of no others. If there is one dread that comes to me more frequently than any other, it is that of losing the power of God. Oh, the agony of having known God's power, of having been used by him, and then having that power withdrawn; to be laid aside as far as any real usefulness is concerned. Men may still praise you, but God can't use you. To see a perishing world around you and to know there is no power in your words to save … wouldn't it be better to die than that?

I have little fear of losing eternal life—every believer has that already. I am in the hand of Jesus Christ and in the hand of God the Father and no one can pluck me out of their hand.[16] But I see so many men from whom God has departed—men once used remarkably by God!—that I walk with fear and trembling, crying out to him daily to keep me from the things that would make the withdrawal of his power necessary. But I am fairly certain that he has made those things plain to me, and I have tried to make them plain to both you and myself in the words I have written here. To sum up, they are these: the surrender of our separation, sin, self indulgence, greed for money, pride, the neglect of prayer and the neglect of the word of God.

Let us, by God's grace, be on our guard against these things from this time on, and in this way guarantee the continuance of God's power in our life and service, until that glad day comes when we can say with Paul, *"I have fought the good fight, I have finished the race, I have kept the faith. Henceforth there is laid up for me the crown of righteousness, which the Lord, the righteous judge, will award to me on that Day,"*[17] or better yet with Jesus, *"I glorified you on earth, having accomplished the work that you gave me to do."*[18]

---

[1] *compare Judges 16:19 and Numbers 6:2, 5*
[2] *1 Samuel 11:6*
[3] *1 Samuel 13:13-14; 15:3, 9-11, 23*
[4] *Psalm 32:1-5; 51:11-13*
[5] *Galatians 5:17*
[6] *1 Corinthians 9:27; Ephesians 5:18*
[7] *2 Timothy 2:3*
[8] *Matthew 17:21*
[9] *1 Timothy 6:10*
[10] *Luke 12:15*
[11] *1 Peter 5:5*
[12] *2 Corinthians 12:7*
[13] *Numbers 20:10-12*
[14] *Mark 5:30*
[15] *Psalm 1:2-3; Joshua 1:8*
[16] *John 10:28-30*
[17] *2 Timothy 4:7-8*
[18] *John 17:4*

Made in United States
Orlando, FL
14 November 2022